My Works,
Ye Mighty

WRITING IN RESIDENCE

ISSN 2818-730X (PRINT) ISSN 2818-7318 (ONLINE)

The Writing in Residence series brings together a diverse range of texts by the artists invited to Athabasca University's Writer in Residence program. Each volume showcases the exceptional talents of these established writers, resulting in works presented in a variety of genres, from essays and personal reflections to memoir, poetry, and conversational interviews. These innovative works provide an opportunity to celebrate contributions made by prominent literary figures and highlight Athabasca University's commitment to fostering literary excellence.

SERIES TITLES

The Virtues of Disillusionment • Steven Heighton | *Indigiqueerness: A Conversation about Storytelling* • Joshua Whitehead, in dialogue with Angie Abdou | *Writing Ukraine* • Myrna Kostash | *My Works, Ye Mighty* • Christian Bök

My Works,

Ye Mighty

Christian Bök

◊ AU PRESS

for
the atom
and
the star

Foreword

Fifteen years ago, in 2010, Athabasca University (AU) welcomed its very first writer to our virtual Writer in Residence program.

Launched with substantial Zoomer support garnered by professor emerita Evelyn Ellerman and shepherded into institutional life under the guidance of Veronica Thompson (then Dean, Faculty of Humanities and Social Sciences), the Writer in Residence program has since been sustained by the resourceful expertise of the program committee. Current members notably include colleagues like acclaimed novelist Angie Abdou and professor Paul Huebener, both of whom have worked with our writers in residence and with AU colleagues to secure ongoing support from Athabasca University and the Canada Council for the Arts. The Writer in Residency program has likewise benefited from the stellar leadership of writing professors here at AU, many of whom have previously served on and chaired the program committee, including Manijeh Mannani, Rumi translator and Dean of the Faculty of Humanities and Social Sciences. Their leadership has kept top writers coming to the program since its inauguration.

The authors who have graced our residency program include well-known, award-winning literati like Myrna Kostash and the late Steven Heighton. Writers in residence have received accolades during their time with us and for work undertaken while in residency, among them: Joshua Whitehead (who in 2021 became the first Indigenous writer to win CBC's Canada Reads) and John Vaillant (who penned much of his book *Fire Weather* while at AU and who went on to become not only a *New York Times* bestseller but also a Pulitzer Prize finalist).

Prior to COVID (the *before times*), our resident authors would make valiant efforts to visit our home community of Athabasca to deliver talks in person to the AU community. We have been honoured and delighted to meet literary luminaries like Tololwa M. Mollel, Tim Bowling, Richard Van Camp, Katherena Vermette, and Esi Edugyan. Despite the occasional technological hiccups, our virtual and hybrid talks have also been well-attended and well-appreciated, including those provided by Hiromi Goto, Anita Rau Badami, Christian Bök, and most recently Bertrand Bickersteth (our resident for 2024–2025).

All our writers have risen to the occasion (and the challenges) of residency at an open, higher education institution. All have proven to be unwaveringly helpful and universally pleasant, both generous and thoughtful — often entertaining. During their residencies, these authors have mentored many members of the AU community, including students, staff, and faculty from across Canada and around the world. These authors have constructively critiqued our community's own creative projects while taking part in engaging interviews and conversations. More recently, AU Press has started publishing work arising from the authors' time with our university as part of the Writing in Residence series.

My Works, Ye Mighty by Christian Bök joins this recently founded book series.

It would be a woeful understatement to say that the poet Christian Bök likes a challenge when it comes to developing an artistic project. Best known for *Eunoia* (2001) — a bestseller in Canada and the UK — Bök occupies a unique rank among poets as a preeminent innovator. No work cements his reputation more thoroughly than the Xenotext project, a dream-haunting work of staggering ambition on which the poet has laboured for decades.

The Xenotext project aims to produce a work of "living poetry" that encodes a poem into the genome of a deathless bacterium named *Deinococcus radiodurans*. (Mark A. McCutcheon, the co-author of this foreword, recalls Bök describing such a mad project in some detail over drinks at the first of Smaro Kamboureli's TransCanada conferences in 2005.) Following publications about this work, like *The Xenotext (Book 1)* in 2015, Bök has achieved some remarkable discoveries and qualified successes. He is the first person in history to write a poem that, when enciphered into the DNA of a life-form, can cause the organism to "write" a poem in response — a poem durable enough to outlive humanity itself.

The writing of a poem into the genome of one of Earth's most unkillable organisms is far out, wilder than science fiction. (How does one cite a bacterium?) To write a poem that might outlast terrestrial civilization puts Bök in the company of ... whom? Of what? Maybe the Voyager probes and their Golden Records? Maybe these probes are the closest comparators to Bök's work — after all, these probes also tackle the most radically existential problems of our posterity, of the vicissitudes of human communication; these probes are, likewise, going to outlast our species in its current, evolutionary phase, perhaps even our planet in its current, geological era.

Bök's expansively imaginative work "cleanses the doors of perception," as William Blake (and The Doors) might put it. Bök's poetry hacks time itself.

Bök's imagination is mythopoetic, his methods seemingly both rigorous and mad, with no shortage of mischievous humour. The Wildean conceit, if not the Ozymandian audacity, of the Xenotext project; the vocabularic acrobatics of his lipograms in *Eunoia*; the deadpan minimalism of his poems about the colour white in *The Kazimir Effect*: all these works show a wicked humour that remains underappreciated, but nevertheless quintessential, in Bök's astonishing body of work. Perhaps the wit comes through clearer in his commentary, in his talks about his writing process and about his artistic purpose. (In light of a thing like the Xenotext, take this book's title, for instance, with however big a grain of salt as you wish.) We are delighted to present, for you, Bök's further words on the work of writing — together with his new writing!

Let us, then, not look on Bök's works as so mighty that they might make us, in our own endeavours, despair — instead, let us celebrate them for their extraordinary reach, their tilting at infinity, their capability to inspire emergent writers and avid readers alike to think as beautifully as angels, if not to dream as big as the cosmos itself.

ADIEN DUBBELBOER *and* MARK A. MCCUTCHEON
Writer in Residence Program Committee, Faculty of Humanities and Social Sciences,
Athabasca University

My Works, Ye Mighty

My Works,
Ye Mighty

Let rivals frown and sneer if, like a king,
I stamp my passions on all lifeless things;

my final words outlasting all these foes,
for whom my epitaph has bred despair;

this anthem seeded in each algal bloom,
sown long ago to yield a plinth of reefs;

or sealed within a patch of shale to save
from loss the fossils of each coelacanth;

or traced upon a mudflat, like the tracks
of ichthyoids that scuffled from the surf;

each phrase a symbol pressed into a fern
safekept within the coal beds of a marsh;

or dipped in amber, like each damselfly,
whose twitches ended in a dab of pitch;

or etched into the claystone from a creek,
where phytosaurs, inhaling lava, thrashed.

I reigned among the graves of pithecines,
whose femurs, broken, lay upon the veldt;

my god unmet, yet scrimshawed in a tusk
to poach the gravid magick from a witch;

each totem chafed into the gabbro bluffs
by bushmen born to hunt the thylacines;

each ochre stain, begored, evoking droves
of boars on frescoes in these humid caves;

or styled in russet glyphs upon the frieze
of cliffs along the miles of jungle growth;

or daubed with fat and ash upon the walls
of grottos where, torchlit, the horses leapt;

these words a dirge among the megaliths,
all lifted, like my crown, to ring the heath;

my masterwork encrypted in these nicks
and kerfs, incut on bricks from ziggurats.

I signed cartouches framed upon facades
of plasterwork, ensconced in mastabahs;

then carved a sign upon the tortoiseshell,
which pyromancers flung into the flames;

the slabs of mud, unbaked until the mobs
that sacked my palace set the tiles ablaze;

the scrolls of vellum, buried, like a hoard
of shekels, stockpiled near a lake of brine;

the condor and the jackal, both displayed
among the laneways raked into the plain;

my battlements that spanned a hinterland
to keep at bay the warlords of the steppe;

my papal hymns, like psalms of seraphim
who kissed the vaulted ceiling in a shrine;

the secret things, unspoken by the bride,
whose grin implied the ruses of a sphinx.

I ruled astride two trunkless legs of stone,
half sunk, obtrusive, in vast seas of sand;

my shattered visage, like a mask that four
colossi wore while staring from the bluff;

my relics left, untouched, inside the crypt
beneath the subfloors of a humble school;

or packed, like keepsakes, in my cylinder
interred below the fairgrounds of a park;

or crated, like ceramic shields, all stacked
and shelved inside the salt cave of a mine;

the organ pipes at mass, intoning drones
with treadles stuck for decades at a time;

each tune in sync with cupronickel gears
that clocked the kiloyears inside my vault;

the massive carving on the mountainside:
out for a walk, my darling — be back soon.

I roamed, alone, toward my cosmodrome
of monuments in the barrens of the west;

a zone where onyx blocks and iron spikes
defended toxic tombs from future ghouls;

the xenon atoms strewn, like dots of dew,
to form three clues upon a nickel plaque;

each cryptograph enciphered, like a gene
that masterminds implanted in a germ;

or etched, like microfiche, upon the sheet
of glass, which soared aboard my satellite;

or mapped inside the disco balls of brass,
which spun in orbit for ten million years;

the bootprints in the moon dust at the site,
where rocketeers unfurled my oriflamme;

my doombook stashed inside a supercar,
whose dummy pilot drove around a star.

I wrote refrains ingrained in metal moons
that oversaw, from space, a storm of rust;

the harmattan in realms where charlatans
mistook a mountain for my countenance;

the folklore in a world of books, all stored
aboard the landers lost among the dunes;

or minted, like a diamond centime, tossed
upon the ice, where rills of ethane pooled;

or etched into my disk of gold, dispatched
beyond the doldrums of the astral squall;

my sketches of two nudes upon the plates
held fast to probes outcast from paradise;

my thrill for eighty seconds from the flash
of static, heard but once, then never since;

a supergiant, dimmed as though eclipsed
by shadow-plays backlit against its blaze.

I raised my mighty screen around each sun
to bend these beams of daylight to my will;

the stars displayed, as though by demigods,
to draw the shapes of either swans or lyres;

each galaxy a wreath immersed in flames,
bequeathed to me, to rest upon my brow;

the trumpets of my fame, as loud as floods
of space-time from the brightest abattoirs;

all superclusters hauled, like cinderblocks,
to build a wall, which framed my universe;

the faint hello in shock waves from a glow
of pride, subsiding since the birth of time;

behold! — the poets who have yet to prove
their lastingness resent what life contrives,

insisting that their jeers are more sublime
than endless deserts, seized by me for art.

Alas, these peers who strive to know me fail,
unless they first surpass what I have dreamt.

εἰ δέ τις εἰδέναι βούλεται πηλίκος εἰμι καὶ
ποῦ κεῖμαι, νικάτω τι τῶν ἐμῶν ἔργων.

A Zoom Lens for The Future of The Text

The Microcosm
of Conceptualism

A IS FOR ATOM
IMAGE BY CHRISTIAN BÖK

01.

Conceptualists have distinguished themselves as poets in part because they explore what I call the "limit-cases" of writing, taking an interest in the most marginal extremes of expression. Some of us, for example, have investigated the limit-cases of "scale" in poetics, composing poems not only as puny as molecules of sugar at the atomistic scale of our DNA, but also as vast as databases of email at the archivist scale of the National Security Agency (NSA).[1] Even though "scale," as a value, has received only the merest notice in the history of poetics, I believe that a sense of scale (be it in degree, in volume, in length) remains crucial to us if we wish to understand the fundamental perspective of poets, who must often adopt a position with respect to their own "unit" of composition — a unit that, whatever its scale, must act like an "atom," recopied and adjoined to make a text.

MAGNIFICATION OF A FULL STOP
IMAGE BY CHRISTIAN BÖK

02.

Consider, for example, the following whimsical speculation about "scale," knowing that, if marked on paper, and if viewed from an extreme vantage of distance, the period at the far end of this sentence might constitute a point of zero dimension; but as I magnify this dot of punctuation, the period soon becomes a circle, with two dimensions; and as I magnify the period even further, zooming into it, I see that the circle becomes a planar fabric of linear fibres, each of which, from afar, has one dimension; and as I magnify each strand further, I see that, eventually, it becomes a tubule, with three dimensions — leading me to conclude that the period at the far end of this sentence might, in fact, occupy a diverse variety of dimensions, each of which contradicts the others, depending upon the scale at which I might prefer to observe such a tiny mark after this last word.

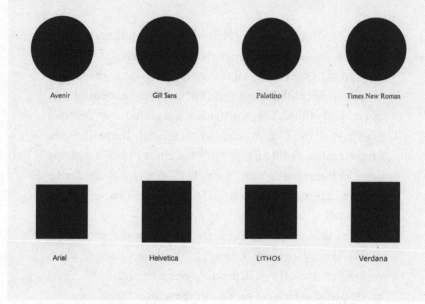

SAMPLES FROM *TYPOGRAPHY OF THE PERIOD*
BY HEIDI NELSON
IMAGE BY CHRISTIAN BÖK

03.

Heidi Neilson in *Typography of the Period* (from 2003) has, in fact, magnified periods from twenty-six different typefaces, "blowing up" each of these atoms of punctuation by 3,000 per cent in order to examine their shapes more closely. Among the samples studied by Neilson, only the periods from typefaces like Avenir, Gill Sans, Palatino, and Times New Roman look like perfect circles, whereas the periods from typefaces like Arial, Helvetica, Lithos, and Verdana look like squarish polygons.[2] The diverse designs for these silhouettes of edgy daubs and oval blots might seem surprising, given the presumable simplicity of the shape for such punctuation — and yet the reader encounters a plethora of forms, not unlike spores of pollen. Her project reminds me of "microdots" used by spies to convey stolen covert documents, miniaturized to the size of a period.

MICROPHOTOGRAPH PORTRAIT OF NICÉPHORE NIÉPCE
BY EMANUEL GOLDBERG
IMAGE BY SCIENCE MUSEUM, LONDON

04.

Emanuel Goldberg (in 1925) actually perfects the technology for making microdots, doing so by using a luminous projector that passes light through a Zeiss microscope fitted with specially corrected lenses, all mounted on an optic bench (cushioned against ambient, seismic vibration), with the image developed on a brass plate coated in a sensitive collodion emulsion of silver chloride and citric acid.[3] Goldberg first makes a microdot that depicts a cameo of Nicéphore Niépce (the pioneer of photography), but eventually Goldberg prints small texts with letters, one micron in size – a resolution equivalent to the microscopic inscription of fifty Bibles per square inch. His techniques drive subsequent innovation in micrography – the modern limits of which include the tunnelling microscope, whose scans can map the contours of a lone atom of hydrogen.

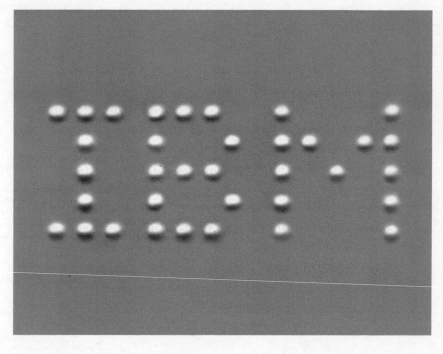

IBM IN XENON ATOMS
IMAGE BY IBM ALMADEN RESEARCH CENTER

05.

Don Eigler at IBM (in 1989) deploys such a tunnelling microscope to position thirty-five atoms of xenon on a plate of cooled nickel so that, by spelling out the trigram for the company, these dots of matter actually comprise the smallest artifact so far manufactured by humanity.[4] Eigler has gone on to draw the kanji glyph for the word *atom* by arranging atomic pixels of iron on a sheet of cooled copper; moreover, he has arrayed molecules of carbon monoxide on a metal panel, so as to write a waggish comment, measurable in nanometres: "If you can read this, you are too close."[5] Such techniques of microscopic inscription (using the tiniest of all periods) has given IBM the power to store one bit of digitizable information in no more than a dozen atoms at a time, thereby increasing the possible capacity for storage of data upon the metallic surfaces of microchips.

CULTURE OF D. RADIODURANS
IMAGE BY CHRISTIAN BÖK

06.

Patrick Chung Wong has, in turn, noted that, in a world of fragile media with limited space to store increasing quantities of data, the atomic domain of DNA might permit us to preserve our cultural heritage against the threat of planetary disasters (including thermonuclear warfare and astrophysical barrage). Wong has illustrated this hypothesis by encoding the lyrics to "It's a Small World (After All)," implanting this song, as a genetic plasmid, inside the chromosome of an extremophile called *Deinococcus radiodurans* — a germ able to survive, without mutation, in even the most lethal of biomes, including the vacuum of outer space.[6] Such "genetic writing" shows the degree to which geneticists have now become poets in the medium of life, storing extensive libraries of data, like microdots for retrieval, inside the genomes of immortal microbes.

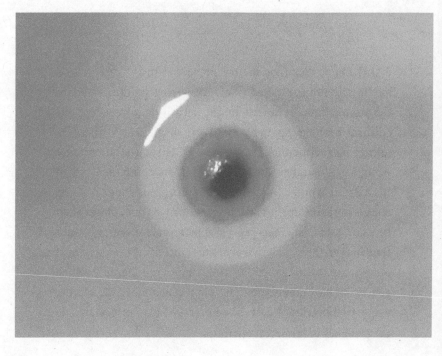

CELLULE OF M. LABORATORIUM
IMAGE BY J. CRAIG VENTER INSTITUTE

07.

Craig Venter (in 2010) has used automated chemistry to create a bespoke species of synthetic bacterium: *Mycoplasma laboratorium* (otherwise nicknamed "Synthia") — a cell bred with an artificially manufactured genome, built from scratch by a computer. Venter has "watermarked" this genome by encoding into it a line from *A Portrait of the Artist as a Young Man* by James Joyce: "To live, to err, to fall, to triumph, to recreate life out of life!"[7] Venter has thus preserved a line of modern, poetic text in the first cells of an embryonic ecosystem, and his experiments have informed my own ongoing project entitled *The Xenotext*, in which I have created an example of "living poetry" by engineering a deathless bacterium so that it becomes not only a durable archive for storing a poem, but also an operant machine for writing a poem — an epic text that might outlast us all.

Ink on a 5.5 by 9 inch substrate of 60-pound offset matte white paper. Composed of: varnish (soy bean oil [$C_{57}H_{98}O_6$], used as a plasticizer: 52%. Phenolic modified rosin resin [Tall oil rosin: 66.2%. Nonylphenol [$C_{15}H_{24}O$]: 16.6%. Formaldehyde [CH_2O]: 4.8%. Maleic anhydride [C_4H_2O3]: 2.6%. Glycerol [C3H8O$_3$]: 9.6%. Traces of alkali catalyst: 0.2%]: 47%): 53.7%. 100S Type Alkyd used as a binder (Reaction product of linseed oil: 50.7%. Isophthalic acid [$C_8H_6O_4$]: 9.5%. Trimethylolpropane [$CH_3CH_2C(CH_2OH)_3$]: 4.7%. Reaction product of tall oil rosin: 12.5%. Maleic anhydride [$C_4H_2O_3$]: 2.5%. Pentaerythritol [$C_5H_{12}O_4$]: 5%. Aliphatic C14 Hydrocarbon: 15%): 19.4%. Carbon Black (C: 92.8%. Petroleum: 5.1%. With sulfur, chlorine, and oxygen contaminates: 2.1%), used as a pigmenting agent: 18.6%. Tung oil (Eleostearic acid [$C_{18}H_{30}O_2$]: 81.9%. Linoleic acid [$C_{18}H_{32}O_2$]: 8.2%. Palmitic acid [$C_{16}H_{32}O_2$]: 5.9%. Oleic acid [$CH_3(CH_2)_7CH=CH(CH_2)_7COOH$]: 4.0%.), used as a reducer: 3.3%. Micronized polyethylene wax (C_2H_4)N: 2.8%. 3/50 Manganese compound, used as a through drier: 1.3%. 1/25 Cobalt linoleate compound used as a top drier: 0.7%. Residues of blanket wash (roughly equal parts aliphatic hydrocarbon and aromatic hydrocarbon): 0.2%. Adhered to: cellulose [$C_6H_{10}O_5$] from softwood sulphite pulp (Pozone Process) of White Spruce (65%) and Jack Pine (35%): 77%; hardwood pulp (enzyme process pre-bleach Kraft pulp) of White Poplar (aspen): 15%; and batch treated PCW (8%): 69.3%. Water [H_2O]: 11.0%. Clay [Kaolinite form aluminum silicate hydroxide ($Al_2Si_2O_5[OH]_4$): 86%. Calcium carbonate ($CaCO_3$): 12%. Diethylenetriamine: 2%], used as a pigmenting filler: 8.4%. Hydrogen peroxide [H_2O_2], used as a brightening agent: 3.6%. Rosin soap, used as a sizer: 2.7%. Aluminum sulfate [$Al_2(SO_4)$]: 1.8%. Residues of cationic softener (H_2O: 83.8%. Base [Stearic acid ($C_{18}H_{36}O_2$): 53.8%. Palmitic acid ($C_{16}H_{32}O_2$): 29%. Aminoethylethanolamine (H_2-NC$_2$-H$_4$-NHC$_2$-H$_4$-OH): 17.2%]: 10.8%. Sucroseoxyacetate: 4.9%. Tallow Amine, used as a surfactant: 0.3%. Sodium chloride [NaCl], used as a viscosity controlling agent: 0.2%) and non-ionic emulsifying defoamer (sodium salt of dioctylsulphosuccinate [$C_{20}H_{37}NaO_7S$]), combined: 1.7%. Miscellaneous foreign contaminates: 1.5%.

FACT
BY CRAIG DWORKIN

08.

Conceptualism must delve into this kind of molecular substrate for poetry, taking a cue, perhaps, from a poem like "Fact" by Craig Dworkin (who lists, exhaustively, all the chemicals in the very page of inked paper used to document the list itself — so that, in fact, the poem "Fact" must vary with each instantiation, since the constituents in the brands of inked paper change from publisher to publisher).[8] I might note that, despite the myopia of critics who feel obliged to dismiss the merits of such outlandish literature, the act of addressing this atomic degree of expression nevertheless constitutes one of the outlying horizons for the future of poetry. I believe that the acuity of our "vision" in poetry depends, in part, upon our ability to "zoom" across a multitude of unexplored dimensions, focusing upon each of them before ever reaching the finality of a full stop.

To Zoom from
an Atom to a Star

SERIES OF SCENES FROM *COSMIC VIEW*
BY KEES BOEKE
IMAGE BY CHRISTIAN BÖK

09.

Kees Boeke in his essay *Cosmic View* (from 1957) conveys the size of the cosmos via a series of images, each scaled up by a power of ten across forty jumps in viewpoint: from a sodium nucleus (at 10^{-13} m) to a galaxy cluster (at 10^{26} m). Boeke depicts a scene, situated at the scale of a Dutch child, holding a cat in her lap while seated in the yard of her school in Bilthoven, near Utrecht.[9] Boeke devotes one page to each jump, "zooming away" from her hand, past a city, a star, a nebula, until reaching a cosmic limit, then "zooming down" into her hand, past a mite, a cell, a virion, until reaching an atomic limit. Boeke places the child in a *mise en abyme*, whose levels of recursive reframing (distanced, then magnified) almost recall the Droste effect, seen in the image of a Dutch nurse, shown at two varied scales, one nested in the other, on packages of Droste cocoa.

SERIES OF SCENES FROM *COSMIC ZOOM*
BY EVA SZASZ
IMAGE BY CHRISTIAN BÖK

10.

Cosmic View has, in turn, inspired the beautiful, haunting photo-play *Cosmic Zoom*, illustrated in 1968 for the National Film Board of Canada by Eva Szasz, who animates the essay by Kees Boeke, zooming from the scale of a proton to the scale of a galaxy in the span of eight minutes. Szasz depicts a Canadian juvenile rowing a boat on the Ottawa River,[10] and much like Boeke in his essay, she also zooms away from the hand of the boy, rising into the atmosphere, passing vast spirals of stars, until reaching a pancosmic perspective; then the animator zooms down into the hand of the boy, diving into a hematocyte, passing tiny helices of atoms, until reaching a subatomic perspective. Szasz places the child in a *mise en abyme*, whose recursive reframing oscillates between two voids — two blots of black space, each one like a full stop at either end of a palindrome.

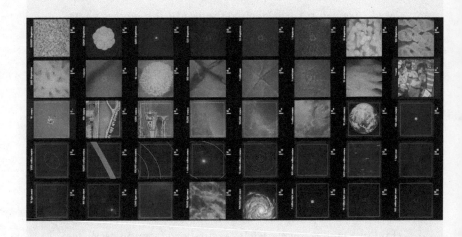

SERIES OF SCENES FROM *POWERS OF TEN*
BY THE EAMES OFFICE
IMAGE BY CHRISTIAN BÖK

11.

Cosmic View has, likewise, inspired the movie *Powers of Ten* produced in 1977 by the designers at the Eames Office, all of whom animate the essay by Kees Boeke, traversing cosmic scales, from 10^{-6} angstroms to 10^{8} light-years. The designers depict a couple picnicking at Burnham Park near Soldier Field in Chicago, and again, like Boeke, the designers zoom away from the hand of a man, asleep, the view moving upward, until reaching the very edge of all observable *galaxiae*; and then the designers zoom down into the hand of the man, asleep, the view moving inward, until reaching the very edge of all observable *minutiae*.[11] The nested frames of squares demarcate each magnitude traversed, receding or widening, as the film undergoes its recursions (hinting perhaps at the Droste effect, if we choose to mistake the film itself for the dream of the picnicker).

SERIES OF SCENES FROM *ZOOM*
BY ISTVÁN BÁNYAI
IMAGE BY CHRISTIAN BÖK

12.

István Bányai in his book *Zoom* offers a rejoinder to all these precedents, depicting a series of images in which every view recedes from a prior view, even as our frames of reference collapse into each other: for example, we see that as the "zoom" proceeds from its initial vantage of a chicken being observed by children in a house, the expanding viewpoint shows this farmyard to be a model scene of toys depicted on the cover of a magazine held in the hand of a boy asleep on the deck of a cruise vessel, now depicted in an ad on the side of a bus, as seen upon the television of a desert cowboy, whose image appears upon the postage for a letter, which is received by a tribesman on a remote island, overflown by an aviator, whose airplane vanishes into the distance as our viewpoint recedes further into outer space, leaving our planet behind, like a full stop.[12]

LOGARITHMIC ILLUSTRATION
OF THE OBSERVABLE UNIVERSE
BY PABLO CARLOS BUDASSI

13.

Each of these "zooms" depicts the act of recursive reframing as a kind of "fall," either a "falling away" (as if pushed from a receding point), or a "falling into" (as if pulled down a swelling abyss). Each of us might undergo a sense of vertigo during this zoom through the void, since we traverse boundless distances via superluminal acceleration, typically forbidden by the laws of physics. With the fall of such a zoom in mind, let me display some of the conceivable, dimensional limits for the minimal element of composition in poetry. For me, at least, all concepts of poetry depend upon a premise about this unit (or "atom"), which poets must recopy and adjoin. I believe that every literary movement teaches a poet to commit to the value of a minimal element in writing, and this unit provides the standard for the scale at which any literary creation can occur.

The Minimal Element
of Writing

THE MARK
IMAGE BY CHRISTIAN BÖK

14.

Jacques Derrida claims that the *mark* constitutes the minimal element of writing — what he calls "the irreducible atom"[13] at the asemic origin for the metaphysics of meaning itself (be this origin in the biogenetic code of life or the cybernetic code of data). The writing of the mark, the *grapheme*, underpins the transmission of information, even before the advent of our phonetic language (for which the mark might seem to constitute the written glyph that evolves to capture an uttered sound). Each extant mark refers, beyond itself, to an absent mark, alluding to this absence, again and again, via iteration and recursion, doing so through a series of sequential references, none of which can terminate in a last mark. The meaning of a mark thus finds itself characterized both by a *differing* across sites of signification and by a *deferring* across times of signification.[14]

THE LETTER
IMAGE BY CHRISTIAN BÖK

15.

Zoom out. Isidore Isou claims, however, that the *letter* itself constitutes the minimal element of writing — what he calls "the fraction of the word"[15] from which "[e]verything must be revealed"[16] (i.e., the asemic pieces of words, pulverized into their alphabetical constituents). Isou insists that these "particles of the Letterist"[17] can revivify the abstract meanings of poetry by confronting the reader with the concreteness of such indivisible foundations for expression in the debris from the destruction of the word. Such a fixation upon the irreducibility of the letter eventually leads Isou, late in life, to formulate an imaginary aesthetic movement called *excoördisme* — a movement, both "extensible" and "co-ordinate," aspiring to become an "art of the infinitely large and the infinitely small"[18] — an art whose concepts transect all scales of expression, from atoms to stars.

THE SYLLABLE
IMAGE BY CHRISTIAN BÖK

16.

Zoom out. Charles Olson claims that the *syllable* constitutes the minimal element of writing — what he calls "the smallest particle of all," situated at "the place of the elements," of the "minims of language" — these "particles of sound," each like a lone note of music.[19] Olson insists that the syllable represents, for him, the "source of speech" — a "minimum" that underpins the euphony of poetry; and consequently, he argues that poets must attend to the juxtaposition of syllables (rather than to the orchestration of either rhyme or metre).[20] He argues, in effect, that lines of verse must consist, at first, of syllables, each one a point of sound, and together these lines produce a "field" of composition (possibly implying that a syllable is a zero dimension, from which the higher orders of both a one-dimensional line and a two-dimensional text might arise).

fall

THE WORD
IMAGE BY CHRISTIAN BÖK

17.

Zoom out. Ferdinand de Saussure claims that, despite his own dubiety about its atomic status, the *word* (as a value) resembles the minimal element of writing — what he calls "the linguistic unit"[21] (i.e., "something central in the mechanism of language"[22]). Saussure suggests that, even though the "concrete entities"[23] of language might prove difficult to delimit, what he calls the "word-unit"[24] seems, nevertheless, to serve as the most convenient touchstone for the "signifier" of the "signified" in writing. The word, for him, offers itself easily as the most standard currency of exchange within language, since the word behaves much like "a one-franc piece,"[25] insofar as every given word denotes a value with respect to the value of every other word. The word, for him, thus functions as a kind of coin in a system of differences, all in reciprocal opposition to each other.

to fall,

for ever and no w
Her eyes had called
to err, to fall, to triu
d appeared to him, t
om the fair courts c

THE PHRASE
IMAGE BY CHRISTIAN BÖK

18.

Zoom out. Jean-François Lyotard claims that the *phrase* constitutes the minimal element of writing — "[t]he only one that is indubitable [...], because it is immediately presupposed"[26] as the most basic of links, to which a genre of both rules and goals might apply. Lyotard argues that the phrase exists to enable an *addressor* to convey *meanings* about a *referent* to an *addressee* (although none of these roles in such a quadrivium can precede the phrase itself, since they emerge only within relation to each other at the moment when the phrase gets articulated).[27] Each phrase follows a set of both customs and motives — but this regimen varies from phrase to phrase such that, when linked, each phrase finds itself articulated in a series of heterogenous, if not incompatible, protocols, all in dispute with each other, unable to reach steady states of signification.

bling. On and on and on and on he strode, far out over the sands, singing wildly to the sea, crying to greet the advent of the life that had cried to him.

Her image had passed into his soul for ever and no word had broken the holy silence of his ecstasy. Her eyes had called him and his soul had leaped at the call. **To live, to err, to fall, to triumph, to recreate life out of life!** A wild angel had appeared to him, the angel of mortal youth and beauty, an envoy from the fair courts of life, to throw open before him in an instant of ecstasy the gates of all the ways of error and glory. On and on and on and on!

He halted suddenly and heard his heart in the silence. How far had he walked? What hour was it?

There was no human figure near him nor any sound borne to him over the air. But the tide was near the turn and already the day was on the wane. He turned landward and ran towards the shore and, running up the sloping beach, reckless of the sharp shingle, found a sandy nook amid a ring of tufted sandknolls and lay down there that the peace and silence of the evening might still the riot of his blood.

THE SENTENCE
IMAGE BY CHRISTIAN BÖK

19.

Zoom out. Ron Silliman claims that, on the contrary, the *sentence* must constitute the minimal element of writing — what he calls the "unit of any literary product" such that "[a]ny further sub-division would leave one with an unusable [...] fragment."[28] Silliman argues that because infants, when learning language, can imitate the contours of a sentence long before they can parse it into subunits, "the sentence is in some sense a primary unit of language."[29] He suggests that "[t]*he sentence is the horizon*, the border between [...] two fundamentally distinct types of integration":[30] one grammatical, one syllogistic — the sentence acting as a "hinge unit" between rules of syntax and rules of reason. The sentence thus provides the standard currency of exchange across orders of meaning, converting a fund of unusable fragments into the coin of tradable arguments.

bling. On and on and on and on he strode, far out over the sands,
singing wildly to the sea, crying to greet the advent of the life that
had cried to him.

Her image had passed into his soul for ever and no word had
broken the holy silence of his ecstasy. Her eyes had called him and
his soul had leaped at the call. To live, to err, to fall, to triumph, to
recreate life out of life! A wild angel had appeared to him, the angel
of mortal youth and beauty, an envoy from the fair courts of life,
to throw open before him in an instant of ecstasy the gates of all the
ways of error and glory. On and on and on and on!

He halted suddenly and heard his heart in the silence. How far
had he walked? What hour was it?

There was no human figure near him nor any sound borne to him
over the air. But the tide was near the turn and already the day was
on the wane. He turned landward and ran towards the shore and,
running up the sloping beach, reckless of the sharp shingle, found a
sandy nook amid a ring of tufted sandknolls and lay down there that
the peace and silence of the evening might still the riot of his blood.

He felt above him the vast indifferent dome and the calm pro-
cesses of the heavenly bodies: and the earth beneath him, the earth
that had borne him, had taken him to her breast.

THE PARAGRAPH
IMAGE BY CHRISTIAN BÖK

20.

Zoom out. Alexander Bain claims that the *paragraph* constitutes the minimal element of writing — what he calls a "division of discourse": i.e., a main unit of thought, defined by its "unity of purpose" (in a manner that recalls the rigour of the poetic stanza).[31] Bain argues that the paragraph integrates otherwise disparate sentences, all of which must unite to develop a single thesis about a topic made prominent in the first of its sentences;[32] hence, the paragraph possesses a "unity" that does not digress from a single stated topic, but that instead elaborates upon a theme in cogent detail. I might note that because the paragraph takes on the properties of a small essay (complete with topical preface, logical comment, and summary closure), paragraphs in an essay partake of the Droste effect (like a fractal), imitating, in miniature, the whole of which they are a piece.

THE PAGE
IMAGE BY CHRISTIAN BÖK

21.

Zoom out. John Trimbur claims that the *page* constitutes the minimal element of writing — what he calls the "unit of discourse" (i.e., "the fundamental feature of print culture," its structural uniformity providing a metric for the length, if not the labour, of writing itself).[33] The page of the modern moment constitutes a kind of *terra nullius*, overwritten with the features of a grid, otherwise invisible, but rule-bound by industrialized typographical norms, complete with uniform fonts in uniform lines, all arrayed in ranks on a sheet of paper, fixed in scale throughout the depth of a sheaf. The page represents a measure for the text, providing countable intervals for the routine of writing, with each turn of the page leading a person not only deeper into the dimensions of the book but also deeper into the dimensions of the self, cultivating an "inwardness" of escape.[34]

THE BOOK
IMAGE BY CHRISTIAN BÖK

22.

Zoom out. Stéphane Mallarmé claims that the *book*, in fact, constitutes the minimal element of writing, "that when all is said and done there is only one, unwittingly attempted by whoever has written" — its unity, in the end, encompassing the world, so as to become "the orphic explanation of the Earth":[35] i.e., "all earthly existence must ultimately be contained in a book."[36] Mallarmé imagines that, in its singularity, such a book is a cosmos unto itself, and each poet can only ever hope to express a fragment of its entirety, aspiring, at best, to realize this "book-to-come" through the book that the poet has at hand to make. I might note again that, in such a vision of bookish oneness, we see the spectre of the Droste effect: the book imitates, in miniature, the universe that it inhabits, making of itself a microcosm that contains a facsimile of the macrocosm.

DUBLINERS

by

JAMES JOYCE

LONDON
GRANT RICHARDS LTD.
PUBLISHERS

A Portrait of the Artist
as a Young Man

BY

JAMES JOYCE

NEW YORK
B. W. HUEBSCH
MCMXVI

ULYSSES

by

JAMES JOYCE

SHAKESPEARE AND COMPANY
12, Rue de l'Odéon, 12
PARIS
1922

**FINNEGANS
WAKE**

by
James Joyce

London
Faber and Faber Limited

THE CORPUS
IMAGE BY CHRISTIAN BÖK

23.

Zoom out. Eli Mandel might claim that the *corpus* constitutes the minimal element of writing — what he calls the "life sentence," in which the whole canon of a single writer becomes the main unit for authorial discourse: i.e., "a life *of* words or a life *in* words."[37] Every work written by a poet gets absorbed into such an opus, all "to serve the sentence" (from which no poet gets out on parole). I might note that not even *parole* (à la Ferdinand de Saussure) allows us to escape *langue* altogether, for only the full stop of death ends such a sentence. The demise of the author, complete with any "last word," leaves behind a body of work, a *corpus*, memorialized under a name, both unique and proper, identifying the standard currency of exchange among the living, who must construct for themselves the grandiose tradition of literature out of these indeed large, albeit prime, units of writing.

JAMES JOYCE   GO

UbuWeb
All avant-garde. All the time.

Recent Additions
Film & Video
Sound
Dance
Papers
Historical
Visual Poetry
Conceptual Writing
Contemporary
Aspen Magazine
Outsiders
/ubu Editions
365 Days Project
Bidoun Presents
Ethnopoetics
Electronic Music Resources
UbuWeb Top Tens
Twitter
UbuWeb Radio Stream
UbuRadio App
Resources
Contact

THE ARCHIVE
IMAGE BY KENNETH GOLDSMITH

24.

Zoom out. Kenneth Goldsmith claims that, on the contrary, the *archive* constitutes the minimal element of writing since, as he notes, the digital genesis of textual corpora now results at once in their curated storage, with everything copied and stowed online in automated databases: "writers are plundering these vast warehouses of text," not for "raw material" — "but rather to [. . .] reshape them";[38] moreover, "large-scale" venues for online social engagement (like Google, Facebook, and Instagram), archive all our interactions with their platforms, collating our utterances in a manner that might rival the repositories of surveillance in servers at the NSA. Each text that we publish in an online milieu now results in the creation of a "library" on our behalf, whose filing system records our writing, all of it searchable by algorithms.

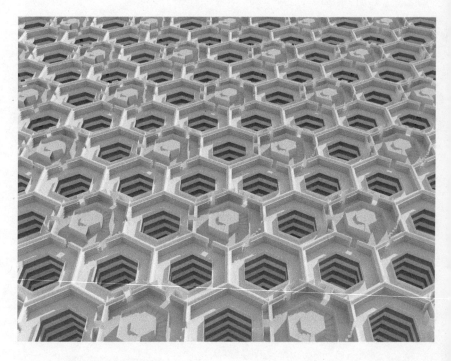

THE LIBRARY OF BABEL
IMAGE BY ALEX WARREN

25.

Zoom out. Jorge Luis Borges imagines the extreme horizon for writing — an archive for every archive: a cosmically exhaustive repository, containing every conceivable permutation of the alphabet (thereby reducing all subsequent authorship to pre-emptive plagiarism). The Library of Babel exhausts the repertoire of language so utterly that "to speak is to fall into tautologies."[39] I might note that such a nightmare already haunts the Conceptualists, who feel a nagging concern that literature might have arisen of its own accord, not from the expressed sentiments of unique authors, but from the automated procedures of formal systems — all of it a fatal order, in which the act of publishing a book is equivalent to the act of unshelving a book, already written, so as to sign your name to its colophon, taking possession of a work first owned by the language itself.

MARK	—	Jacques Derrida
LETTER	—	Isidore Isou
SYLLABLE	—	Charles Olson
PHRASE	—	Jean-François Lyotard
SENTENCE	—	Ron Silliman
PARAGRAPH	—	Alexander Bain
PAGE	—	John Trimbur
BOOK	—	Stéphane Mallarmé
CORPUS	—	Eli Mandel
ARCHIVE	—	Kenneth Goldsmith
BABEL	—	Jorge Luis Borges

THE UNITS OF COMPOSITION
IMAGE BY CHRISTIAN BÖK

26.

Conceptualism suggests that, from the tiny scrawl of aleph to the vast sprawl of Babel, each scale of writing fosters its own poetics about the unit (or "atom") of composition. Disputes among poets might, in fact, arise (at least in part) from disagreement about what constitutes this "true" unit — so that, for example, both the exponents of "lyricist poetry" and the exponents of "concrete poetry" might misjudge the mutual merits of each other, largely because the former poets fixate upon the aptest word (*le mot juste*), as the preferred unit of expression, whereas the latter poets fixate upon the asemic mark (*la signe nue*), as the preferred unit of expression. I might even go so far as to aver that, among schools of writing, Conceptualism has so far explored the most extreme of all units, be they as Lilliputian as small molecules or as elephantine as giant databases.

SUSAN, OUT FOR A PIZZA
BY WIM DELVOYE

27.

Future scales of our civilization might, in fact, offer even more stupendous dimensions for expression, zooming out from the human scale of a handwritten memo to the godly scale of a terraformed moon. We might see the hint of such grandiosity, for example, in the epic work of an artist like Wim Delvoye, who imagines carving his poetry at giant sizes into mountainsides, leaving banal notes for readers everywhere within the vicinity to read from afar: "Susan. Out for a pizza. Back in five minutes. George."[40] We might find ourselves surrounded by samples of such titanic writing, whose units of composition zoom out to vastitudes that graduate from the planetal, from the sidereal, from the galactic, all the way to the infinite — and yet, like an ant that crawls over a letter carved upon a tombstone, we may, in fact, be too puny to read the epitaph that we inhabit.

The Macrocosm
of Conceptualism

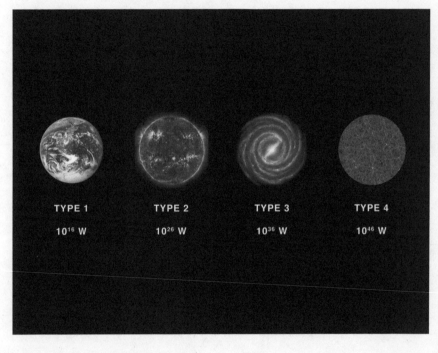

TYPE 1   TYPE 2   TYPE 3   TYPE 4

10^{16} W 10^{26} W 10^{36} W 10^{46} W

THE KARDASHEV SCALE
IMAGE BY CHRISTIAN BÖK

28.

Nikolai Kardashev has categorized civilizations based upon the amount of energy that a civilization can expend (measured in total watts) over its lifetime, each type increasing its usage of power by ten orders of magnitude above its prior stage of development. A Type I civilization can access the energetic potential of an entire planetal system, expending 10^{16} watts in the course of development; a Type II civilization can access the energetic potential of an entire sidereal system, expending 10^{26} watts in the course of development; and a Type III civilization can access the energetic potential of an entire galactic system, expending 10^{36} watts in the course of development.[41] A Type IV civilization (not identified by Kardashev but theorized by others) might conceivably access the energetic potential of an entire cosmos, achieving an almost divine power over the physics of reality itself.

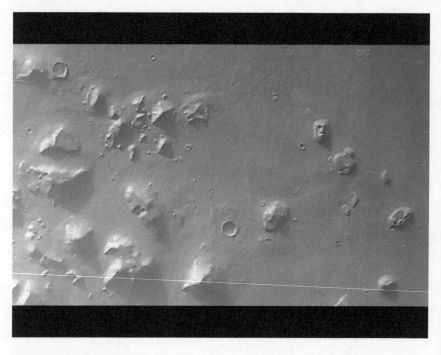

CYDONIA PLANITIA
IMAGE BY NASA JPL

29.

Type I Kardashev civilizations, like ours, might build mega-structures large enough to cover a planet with writing for orbital readers, as suggested in 1826 by Carl Gauss (who proposes to plant wheatfields on tundras so as to convey axioms of geometry to lunar aliens).[42] Just as Percival Lowell might have misperceived *canali* criss-crossing the plains of Mars, mistaking illusory channels for evidence of artificial irrigation during his telescopic monitoring of the planet,[43] so also has Richard C. Hoagland argued that (despite evidence to the contrary from NASA), the Cydonia Planitia on Mars displays evidence of intelligent inscription, including monuments and pyramoids, all arranged in significant geometrical patterns.[44] When zooming into these features with orbital cameras, however, the *pareidolia* of their artificiality disappears into natural geology.

TRANSITING OBJECTS
IMAGE BY LUC ARNOLD

30.

Luc Arnold notes that Type II Kardashev civilizations might build megastructures large enough to occlude the light from their star, producing visible shadows (like trigons or louvres), detectable as "writing" in the transitive light-curve from a luminary backdrop.[45] Tabetha Boyajian has observed that the star KIC 8462852 is, in fact, undergoing such a recurrent expanding occultation so titanic that no phenomenon in Nature can readily explain the light-curve of the ongoing dimming (which has persisted, dipping on one occasion by as much as 22%).[46] Even though a cometary envelope of dust might account for some of these observations, the oddness of the anomaly has, nevertheless, caused some astronomers to indulge in extravagant speculation, suggesting that a Dyson swarm of tiny bots might be engulfing the star so as to capture its entire output of energy.[47]

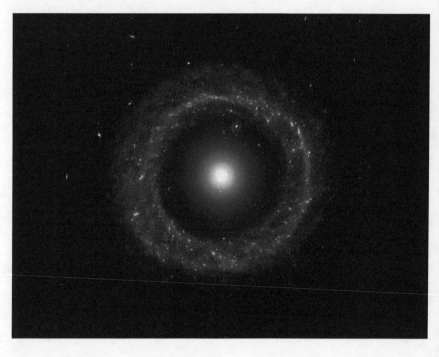

HOAG'S OBJECT
IMAGE BY NASA AND HUBBLE HERITAGE

31

Jaron Lanier notes that Type III Kardashev civilizations might build megastructures large enough to require the reorganization of stellar systems into written symbols (what Lanier calls "graphstellations"), whose inscriptions might span an entire galaxy for eons.[48] Joseph Voros has observed that the galaxy PGC 54559 (otherwise known as Hoag's Object) might constitute such an enigma, insofar as no phenomenon in Nature can readily explain the formation of such a perfect annulus of stars arranged almost exclusively within the radius of habitable distances from the central, radiant core.[49] Even though a collision between two galaxies might account, in part, for this ring (with one galaxy passing through the other, like a bullet passing through a bullseye), no putative galaxies in the region lend support to this hypothesis, thus leading to such speculation.

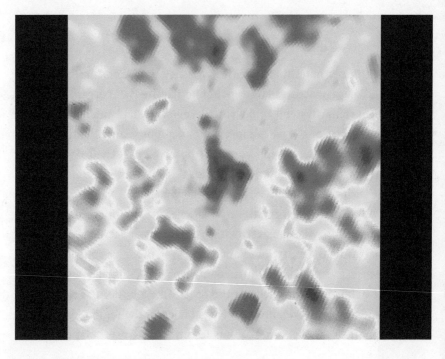

CMB COLD SPOT IN THE ERIDANUS SUPERVOID
IMAGE BY ESA

32.

Stephen Hsu and Anthony Zee have implied that Type IV Kardashev civilizations might go so far as to transmit messages at cosmic scales by adjusting the parameters for the microwave background during the creation of the universe (perhaps encoding up to 100,000 bits of data in the anisotropic fluctuation of temperatures across this panorama), thereby leaving behind an imprimatur upon the structure of the macrocosm.[50] Ruari Mackenzie et al. have observed that the CMB Cold Spot (coincident with the Eridanus Supervoid on the Planck map of the sky) might, in fact, correspond to such a pancosmic signature, because the spot is both so gigantic and so unlikely that no phenomenon in Nature can readily explain its origin, causing Mackenzie et al. to leave open the implication that the void might provide evidence for a parallel universe, entangled with our own.[51]

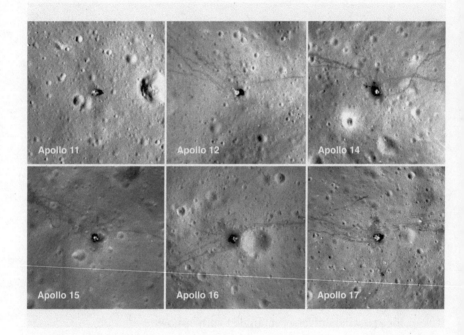

LUNAR SITES OF THE APOLLO MISSIONS
IMAGE BY NASA GSFC

33.

Humanity has only now begun to leave its bootprints and its treadmarks upon the surfaces of other planetoids (like the Moon), and only recently have the Pioneer probes and the Voyager probes begun to pass beyond the heliosphere, exiting our Solar System, while harbouring messages about our earthly culture on plaques and records, so as to address exocivilizations above us on the Kardashev scale. We have only now begun to broadcast messages, via radio waves, into outer space, deliberately transmitting news of our whereabouts to Messier 13 (via the Arecibo Observatory), then later transferring other kinds of information into the void with abandon, including not only an advert for Doritos™, sent to the star HD 95128 in the constellation of Ursa Major, but also the movie *The Day the Earth Stood Still* (starring Keanu Reeves), sent to the star Alpha Centauri.[52]

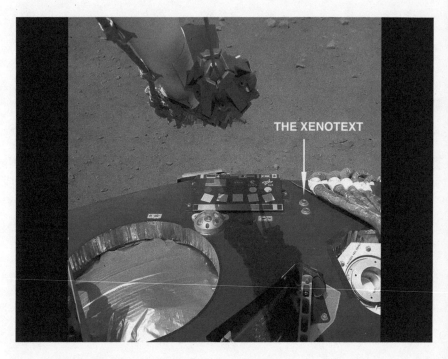

THE XENOTEXT

*THE DECK OF THE INSIGHT LANDER
AT ELYSIUM PLANITIA ON MARS*
IMAGE BY NASA JPL

34.

The Xenotext participates in this legacy of exoplanetary transmission, insofar as my poem constitutes a digital payload aboard a fleet of spacecraft launched by NASA into the void. *The Xenotext* resides, for example, in two microchips within the vicinity of Mars: one aboard the MAVEN probe in orbit around the planet; and one aboard the InSight probe on the Martian surface at Elysium Planitia. *The Xenotext* has also resided in two other microchips: one aboard the OSIRIS-REX probe (visiting the asteroid Bennu); and one aboard the Hayabusa-2 probe (visiting the asteroid Ryugu). The Jamesburg Earth Station in Carmel, California, has also beamed *The Xenotext* to the star Gliese 526 in the constellation of Boötes (5.5 parsecs from Earth), doing so as part of a plan to communicate with any exocivilization that might be orbiting this red dwarf star.

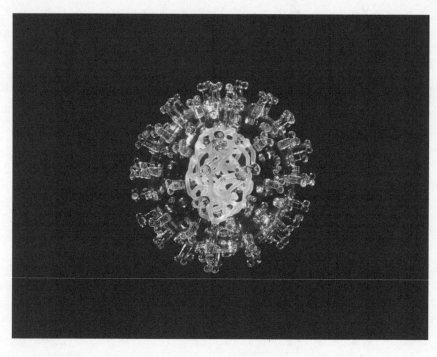

COVID-19
BY LUKE JERRAM

35.

Ultimately, Conceptualism seeks to prepare poetry for a future milieu, where all scales of writing transect each other across an enormous spectrum of dimensions — a milieu perhaps akin to our own emergent dystopia, where a molecular substrate (like the ACE2 receptor on a lung cell) can become the site for microscopic inscription by a coronavirus, whose replication causes every human on Earth to download an app called "Zoom" so that we might interact with each other while quarantined (each of us sharing recorded readings of poetry, broadcast from our prisons of atomized solitude). Conceptualism lets us zoom into the future of poetry, beyond the routinely predicted demise of poetry — a demise upstaged in advance by other cultural concerns more epic than any poem, even one immortalized at the puny scale of an atom or at the vast scale of the void.

Notes

1   *The Xenotext* by Christian Bök encodes a poem as a tiny gene inserted into the chromosome of a bacterium (*E. coli*), whereas *The Hillary Clinton Emails* (an exhibition by Kenneth Goldsmith) reprints the tranche of letters withheld by Hillary Clinton but released by WikiLeaks during the American election of 2016.

2   Neilson, *Typography of the Period*.

3   Goldberg, "A New Process for Microphotography."

4   Browne, "Two Researchers Spell 'IBM,' Atom by Atom."

5   Ganapati, "Twenty Years of Moving Atoms, One by One."

6   Wong, et al., "Organic Data Memory Using the DNA Approach," 97.

7   Gibson, et al., "Creation of a Bacterial Cell Controlled by a Chemically Synthesized Genome," 52–56.

8   Dworkin, "Fact."

9   Boeke, *Cosmic View*, 9.

10 Verrall (dir.), and Szasz (anim.), *Cosmic Zoom*.

11 Eames and Eames, *Powers of Ten*.

12 Bányai, *Zoom*.

13 Derrida, *Of Grammatology*, 9.

14 Derrida, "Différance," 8.

15 Isou, "The Evolution of the Technical Sensibility in Poetry."

16 Isou, "Manifesto of Letterist Poetry," 72.

17 Isou, "The Force Fields of Letterist Painting," 78.

18 Isou, *Manifeste de l'Excoördisme*, 1.

19 Olson, "Projective Verse," 241.

20 Olson, "Projective Verse," 241.

21 Saussure, *Course in General Linguistics*, 103.

22 Saussure, *Course in General Linguistics*, 111.

23 Saussure, *Course in General Linguistics*, 102.

24 Saussure, *Course in General Linguistics*, 94.

25 Saussure, *Course in General Linguistics*, 115.

26 Lyotard, *The Differend: Phrases in Dispute*, xi.

27 Lyotard, *The Differend: Phrases in Dispute*, 14.

28 Silliman, "The New Sentence," 78.

29 Silliman, "The New Sentence," 65.

30 Silliman, "The New Sentence," 87.

31 Bain, *English Composition and Rhetoric*, 91.

32 Bain, *English Composition and Rhetoric*, 112.

33 Trimbur, et al., "The Page as a Unit of Discourse," 94.

34 Trimbur, et al., "The Page as a Unit of Discourse," 112.

35 Mallarmé, "Letter to Paul Verlaine (16 Nov 1885)," 143.

36 Mallarmé, "The Book: A Spiritual Instrument," 80.

37 Mandel, *Life Sentence*, 7.

38 Goldsmith, *Uncreative Writing*, 188.

39 Borges, "The Library of Babel," 86.

40 "Wim Delvoye's Profane Messages Hammered into Rocks in Stunning Scale." See in particular *Swiss Mountain*, 1996.

41 Kardashev, "Transmission of Information by Extraterrestrial Civilizations," 219.

42 "The Moon and Its Inhabitants."

43 Lowell, *Mars and Its Canals*.

44 Hoagland, *The Monuments of Mars: A City on the Edge of Forever*.

45 Arnold, "Transit Light-Curve Signatures of Artificial Objects," 535.

46 Boyajian, et al., "Planet Hunters x. kic 8462852 – Where's the Flux?"

47 Wright, "What Could Be Going on with Boyajian's Star? Part VIII: Alien Megastructures."

48 Lanier, "Rearranging Stars to Communicate with Aliens."

49 Voros, "Galactic-Scale Macro-Engineering: Looking for Signs of Other Intelligent Species."

50 Hsu, and Zee, "Message in the Sky," 2.

51 Mackenzie, et al., "Evidence Against a Supervoid Causing the CMB Cold Spot."

52 Quast, "A Profile of Humanity."

References

"The Moon and Its Inhabitants." *Edinburgh New Philosophical Journal* (Oct 1826): 389–90.

Arnold, Luc F. A. "Transit Light-Curve Signatures of Artificial Objects." *The Astrophysical Journal* 627 (01 Jul 2005): 534–39.

Bain, Alexander. *English Composition and Rhetoric.* D. Appleton and Co., 1890.

Bányai, István. *Zoom.* Viking Press, 1995.

Boeke, Kees. *Cosmic View: The Universe in 40 Jumps.* John Day Co., 1957.

Bök, Christian. *The Xenotext (Book 1).* Coach House Books, 2015.

Borges, Jorge Luis. "The Library of Babel." In *Ficciones.* Trans. Anthony Kerrigan and Anthony Bonner. Grove Press, 1962.

Boyajian, T. S., et al. "Planet Hunters X. KIC 8462852 — Where's the Flux?" *arXiv.org* (26 Jan 2016): 1–17. https://arxiv.org/pdf/1509.03622.pdf.

Browne, Malcolm W. "Two Researchers Spell 'IBM,' Atom by Atom." *The New York Times* (05 Apr 1990): B11.

Delvoye, Wim. 'Swiss Mountain, 1996.' *Public Delivery* (20 Sep 2024): https://publicdelivery.org/wim-delvoye-mountains/.

Derrida, Jacques. "Différance." In *Margins of Philosophy*, 1–28. Trans. Alan Bass. University of Chicago Press, 1982.

Derrida, Jacques. *Of Grammatology.* Trans. Gayatri Chakravorty Spivak. Johns Hopkins University Press, 1974.

Dworkin, Craig. 'Fact.' *Poetry Foundation* (Jul/Aug 2009): https://www.poetryfoundation.org/poetrymagazine/poems/52694/fact-56d23160d463d.

Eames, Charles, and Ray Eames, dir. *Powers of Ten.* Pyramid Films, 1977.

Ganapati, Priya. "Twenty Years of Moving Atoms, One by One." *Wired* (30 Sep 2009): https://www.wired.com/2009/09/gallery-atomic-science/.

Gibson, Daniel G. et al. "Creation of a Bacterial Cell Controlled by a Chemically Synthesized Genome." *Science* 329 (02 Jul 2010): 52–56.

Goldberg, Emanuel. "A New Process for Microphotography." *The British Journal of Photography* 73, no. 13 (13 Aug 1926): 462–65.

Goldsmith, Kenneth. *Uncreative Writing: Managing Language in the Digital Age*. Columbia University Press, 2011.

Hoagland, Richard C. *The Monuments of Mars: A City on the Edge of Forever*. North Atlantic Books, 1987.

Hsu, S., and A. Zee. "Message in the Sky." *arXiv.org* (03 Jun 2006): 1–3. https://arxiv.org/pdf/physics/0510102.pdf.

Isou, Isidore. "The Evolution of the Technical Sensibility in Poetry." In *Introduction to Isidore Isou* by Sam Cooper (26 May 2019): https://situationistresearch.wordpress.com/2019/05/26/intro duction-to-isidore-isou/.

Isou, Isidore. "The Force Fields of Letterist Painting." *Visible Language* 17, no. 3 (1983): 77–78.

Isou, Isidore. *Manifeste de l'Excoördisme ou Du Téïsynisme Mathématique et Artistique*. Éditions Galerie de Paris, 1992.

Isou, Isidore. "Manifesto of Letterist Poetry." *Visible Language* 17, no. 3 (1983): 70–74.

Kardashev, Nikolai. "Transmission of Information by Extraterrestrial Civilizations." *Soviet Astronomy* 8, no. 2 (Sep–Oct 1964): 218–21.

Lanier, Jaron. "Rearranging Stars to Communicate with Aliens." *Discover* (08 Feb 2008): https://www.discovermagazine.com/ the-sciences/rearranging-stars-to-communicate-with-aliens.

Lowell, Percival. *Mars and Its Canals*. Macmillan and Co., 1906.

Lyotard, Jean-François. *The Differend: Phrases in Dispute*. Trans. Georges Van Den Abbeele. University of Minnesota Press, 1988.

Mackenzie, Ruari, et al. "Evidence Against a Supervoid Causing the CMB Cold Spot." *arXiv.org* (12 Apr 2017): 1–12. https://arxiv.org/ pdf/1704.03814.pdf.

Mallarmé, Stéphane. "The Book: A Spiritual Instrument." In *Stéphane Mallarmé: Selected Poetry and Prose*, 80–84. Ed. Mary Ann Caws. New Directions, 1982.

Mallarmé, Stéphane. "Letter to Paul Verlaine (16 Nov 1885)." In *Selected Letters of Stéphane Mallarmé*, 142–48. Ed. Rosemary Lloyd. University of Chicago Press, 1988.

Mandel, Eli. *Life Sentence: Poems and Journals, 1976–1980*. Press Porcépic, 1981.

Neilson, Heidi. *Typography of the Period: A Brief Introduction*. Heidi Neilson, 2003.

Olson, Charles. "Projective Verse." In *Collected Prose*, 239–49. Eds. Donald Allen and Benjamin Friedlander. University of California Press, 1997.

Quast, Paul E. "A Profile of Humanity: The Cultural Signature of Earth's Inhabitants Beyond the Atmosphere." *International Journal of Astrobiology* (15 Aug 2018): 1–21.

Saussure, Ferdinand de. *Course in General Linguistics*. Eds. Charles Bally and Albert Sechehaye. Trans. Wade Baskin. Philosophical Library, 1959.

Silliman, Ron. "The New Sentence." In *The New Sentence*, 63–93. Roof Books, 1987.

Trimbur, John, et al. "The Page as a Unit of Discourse: Notes Toward a Counterhistory of Writing Studies." In *Beyond Postprocess*, 94–113. Eds. Sidney I. Dobrin, J. A. Rice, and Michael Vastola. Utah State University Press, 2011.

Verrall, Robert, dir. *Cosmic Zoom*. National Film Board, 1968.

Voros, Joseph. "Galactic-Scale Macro-Engineering: Looking for Signs of Other Intelligent Species, as an Exercise in Hope for Our Own." *arXiv.org* (28 Nov 2013): 1–17. https://arxiv.org/pdf/1412.4011.pdf.

Wong, Pak Chung, Kwong-kwok Wong, and Harlan Foote. "Organic Data Memory Using the DNA Approach." *Communications of the ACM* 46, no. 1 (Jan 2003): 95–98.

Wright, Jason T. "What Could Be Going on with Boyajian's Star? Part VIII: Alien Megastructures." *Astrowright* (02 Sep 2016): https://sites.psu.edu/astrowright/2016/09/02/what-could-be-going-on-with-boyajians-star-part-viii-alien-megastructures/.

List of Illustrations

13 *Logarithmic Illustration of the Observable Universe.* Image by Pablo Carlos Budassi. License: CC BY-SA 3.0 (Wikipedia).

14 *The Mark.* Image by Christian Bök.

15 *The Letter.* Image by Christian Bök.

16 *The Syllable.* Image by Christian Bök.

17 *The Word.* Image by Christian Bök.

18 *The Phrase.* Image by Christian Bök.

19 *The Sentence.* Image by Christian Bök. License: PDM 1.0 (James Joyce Foundation).

20 *The Paragraph.* Image by Christian Bök. License: PDM 1.0 (James Joyce Foundation).

21 *The Page.* Image by Christian Bök. License: PDM 1.0 (James Joyce Foundation).

22 *The Book.* Image by Christian Bök. License: PDM 1.0 (James Joyce Foundation).

23 *The Corpus.* Image by Christian Bök. License: PDM 1.0 (James Joyce Foundation).

24 *The Archive.* Image by Kenneth Goldsmith. Permission: Kenneth Goldsmith.

25 *The Library of Babel.* Image by Alex Warren. Permission: Alex Warren.

26 *The Units of Composition.* Image by Christian Bök.

27 *Susan, Out for a Pizza.* Image by Wim Delvoye: 1996, Laser inkjet on canvas, 132.5 cm × 196.0 cm. Permission: Studio Wim Delvoye.

28 *The Kardashev Scale.* Image by Christian Bök.

29 *Cydonia Planitia.* Image by the NASA Jet Propulsion Laboratory (NASA JPL). License: PDM 1.0 (NASA JPL).

30 *Transiting Objects.* Image by Luc Arnold. License: CC (American Astrophysical Society). Permission: Luc Arnold.

31 *Hoag's Object.* Image by NASA and Hubble Heritage. License: PDM 1.0 (NASA and Hubble Heritage).

32 CMB *Cold Spot in the Eridanus Supervoid.* Image by the European Space Agency (ESA). Digitally modulated by Christian Bök. License: CC-BY-SA-NC-3.0-IGO (ESA).

33 *Lunar Sites of the Apollo Missions.* Images by the NASA Godard Space Flight Center (NASA GSFC). Digitally modulated by Christian Bök. License: PDM 1.0 (NASA GSFC).

34 *The Deck of the InSight Lander at Elysium Planitia on Mars.* Image by NASA JPL. Digitally modulated by Christian Bök. License: PDM 1.0 (NASA JPL).

35 COVID-19. Glass model and photo by Luke Jerram. Digitally modulated by Christian Bök. Permission: Luke Jerram Ltd.

Acknowledgements

All my projects require much perseverance to complete — and this volume owes its fruition, in part, to the devoted support of patient friends: Angie Abdou, André Alexis, Derek Beaulieu, Gregory Betts, Mikael Brygger, Anthony Etherin, Clara Etherin, Kenneth Goldsmith, Paul Huebener, Ken Hunt, Kathy Killoh, Paul Magee, Manijeh Mannani, Nick Montfort, Simon Morris, Daniela de Paulis, Michael Redhill, et al. Versions of "A Zoom Lens for the Future of the Text" have been presented for events on behalf of the following institutions: the SETI Institute (2023), the University of Canberra (2022), the University of the Arts Helsinki (2021), the Vermont Studio Center (2019), and the University College Dublin (2019). An early draft of "A Zoom Lens for the Future of the Text" has appeared in print at the *Belfield Literary Review* (2021).

Athabasca University has liberally supported the creation of "My Works, Ye Mighty" (and other other poems) during my tenure as the writer in residence for 2023. Without patronage in service to a bold risk, this publication might not have, otherwise, existed.

"My Works, Ye Mighty" constitutes a rejoinder to the famous sonnet "Ozymandias" by Percy Bysshe Shelley (who depicts the ruined statue of Ramesses II, undercutting the hubris of its Pharaonic vainglory). Shelley mocks the presumption of immortality in the inscription on this monument, even though historians in the era of Shelley credit Ramesses II with the invention of libraries (whose caches furnish every civilization with the means to outlast their own demise). My poem suggests that, throughout history, life itself has always wagered its own achievements against gradual erosion by entropy — and I imply that the cosmos itself might embody the godly ruins of such an artistic exercise, no less hubristic than any menhir in the desert. "A Zoom Lens for the Future of the Text" recounts my hope for the endurance of poetry across every scale of existence.

¶ The first edition of *My Works, Ye Mighty* was printed in a limited run of 500 unique copies. The cover image was magnified incrementally to make 500 different versions. The text was set in Borges, a contemporary revival of French Renaissance type design inspired by the work of Jorge Luis Borges. The font was created by Alejandro Lo Celso, first published by PampaType in 2002, and rereleased in 2022.

Christian Bök is the author of *Eunoia* (Coach House Books, 2001), a bestselling work of experimental literature that has won the Griffin Prize for Poetic Excellence (2002). *Crystallography* (Coach House Press, 1994), his first book of poetry, has been nominated for the Gerald Lampert Memorial Award (1995). *Nature* has interviewed Bök about his work on *The Xenotext* (making him the first poet ever to appear in this famous journal of science). Bök has also exhibited artworks derived from *The Xenotext* at galleries around the world; moreover, his poem from this project has hitched a ride, as a digital payload, aboard a number of probes exploring the Solar System (including the InSight lander, now at Elysium Planitia on the surface of Mars). Bök is a Fellow of the Royal Society of Canada, and he teaches at Leeds Beckett University in the UK.

Published by AU Press, Athabasca University
1 University Drive, Athabasca, Alberta T9S 3A3

https://doi.org/10.15215/aupress/ 9781771994347.01

Cover and interior design by Natalie Olsen, kisscutdesign.com
Cover photo © Scott Snyder
Printed and bound in Canada

Library and Archives Canada Cataloguing in Publication
Title: My works, ye mighty / Christian Bök.
Names: Bök, Christian, 1966– author
Description: Series statement: Writing in residence |
   Includes bibliographical references.
Identifiers: Canadiana (print) 20250102242 | Canadiana (ebook)
   20250102315 | ISBN 9781771994347 (softcover) | ISBN
   9781771994354 (PDF) | ISBN 9781771994361 (EPUB)
Subjects: LCGFT: Essays.
Classification: LCC PS8553.O4727 M9 2025 | DDC C814/.54—dc23

We acknowledge the financial support of the Government of
Canada through the Canada Book Fund (CBF) for our publishing
activities and the assistance provided by the Government of
Alberta through the Alberta Media Fund.

Canada   Alberta
        Government